Self-Discovery Questions:
155 Breakthrough Questions
to
Accelerate Massive Action

Barrie Davenport

Disclaimer

No part of this publication may be reproduced or transmitted in any form or by any means, mechanical or electronic, including photocopying or recording, or by any information storage and retrieval system, or transmitted by email without permission in writing from the publisher.

While all attempts have been made to verify the information provided in this publication, neither the author nor the publisher assumes any responsibility for errors, omissions, or contrary interpretations of the subject matter herein.

This book is for entertainment purposes only. The views expressed are those of the author alone, and should not be taken as expert instruction or commands. The reader is responsible for his or her own actions.

Adherence to all applicable laws and regulations, including international, federal, state, and local governing professional licensing, business practices, advertising, and

Your Free Gift

As a way of saying thanks for your purchase, I hope you'll enjoy my free Self-Confidence Test to help you determine where you can make positive changes for improvement and growth. Being a confident person involves all aspects of your life from your relationships to your career. The key is to identify what you want to change in each area and create a plan of action to kickstart a real positive shift.

With this quick test, you'll learn exactly where you need to work on your self-confidence to help you become more successful and positive in your work and personal life. Becoming a more confident person doesn't happen by itself. You can boost your confidence by recognizing the behaviors and thoughts holding you back, and then learning new skills to help improve your motivation and feelings of self-empowerment.

You can download the Self-Confidence Test by going to this site:
http://simpleselfconfidence.com/free-test

Contents

Disclaimer iii

Your Free Gift v

Who Am I? 1

Introduction 3

Self-Awareness 9

Potential 19

Life Priorities 25

Career 31

Finances 39

Confidence and Self-Esteem 45

Life Problems 55

Health 61

Relationships 67

Lifestyle 77

Conclusion 85

Want to Learn More? 91

Did You Like *Self-Discovery Questions*? .. 93

Other Books You Might Enjoy from Barrie Davenport... 95

Who Am I?

My name is Barrie Davenport, and I run two top-ranked personal development sites, **Live Bold and Bloom** and **BarrieDavenport.com.** I'm a certified personal coach, former public relations professional, author, and creator of several online courses on self-confidence, life passion, and habit creation.

My work as a coach, blogger, and author is focused on offering people practical strategies for living happier, more successful, more confident lives. I utilize time-tested, evidence based, action-oriented principles and methods to create real and measurable results for self-improvement.

As a coach, I've learned through countless sessions with courageous, motivated clients that each individual has the answers within them. Every person has the wisdom and intuition to know what is best for themselves. Sometimes we simply need someone or something to coax it out of us and encourage us to move forward.

That's what I hope this book will do for you—help you to move forward to a happier, fuller, and more confident life where you enjoy the success you want to achieve, and live to your fullest potential. Thank you for choosing my book to support you on your journey.

Introduction

*"To be on a quest is nothing more or less
than to become an asker of questions."*

~Sam Keen

One of the most valuable tools I use as a career
and personal coach is questioning.

A probing question presented at the right time can
help a client reach that "aha" moment when the
pieces fall into place for them. Coaches ask a lot of
questions, which might seem like an inquisition to a
new client, but the purpose is not to satisfy the
coach's curiosity or to put the client on the spot. It's
to encourage the client dig more deeply within
themselves to uncover the answer or solution they
are seeking.

Often I'll ask the client a question and sit quietly, waiting for a reply. The silence is awkward, and to fill the uncomfortable gap, the client might answer, "I just don't know." I always follow-up with, "Yes you do." After a few minutes, and further thought, they usually do know. The answer is there all the time. It just takes a good question to help it bubble to the surface.

Most people don't take the time or have the inclination to ask themselves penetrating questions. In fact, it can be pretty uncomfortable when you start poking around your psyche and looking underneath the hood. There are some questions that expose wounds too raw to explore and mend without the support of a trained counselor.

However, there are many questions that reveal the uncharted territory of your nature, buried desires, and motivations. Once you rummage deeper into these unexamined areas, you can find gems and sometimes goldmines that lead to profound changes or simply daily improvements or redirection.

Working with a coach is the most efficient way to learn about yourself and how to reach your dreams. But you can still coach yourself using powerful questions to help uncover what's most important and meaningful to you and to facilitate inner growth and positive action.

Self-questioning is a powerful tool for self-awareness that forces us to pause from reactive or automatic behaviors and to think deeply about ourselves and our beliefs. In fact, sometimes they challenge our beliefs about what we "know" to be true.

As a coach, I use thoughtful questions to help clients elicit new insights, uncover buried dreams, and reach conclusions about who they are and what they want for their lives. Often when I ask a question, the first comment is one of surprise—"Wow, that's a great question. I've never thought about that." As the client ponders the question, the subconscious mind goes into action, and often small breakthroughs and "aha" moments are the result.

One of my own "aha" moments happened during a particularly stressful and confusing time when my sister asked me the question, "What would happen if you just let go and allowed the universe to catch you?" In essence, she was asking what would happen if I stopped fretting and trying to control events and simply let life unfold?

It was a profound moment for me, as it forced me to realize two things. First, my stress and worry wouldn't change the way life happens. Also, I realized if I did let go of control, I wouldn't die. Nothing would happen that I couldn't cope with in the moment. The only control I have is over my own reactions.

Fortunately, you can trigger these insightful moments for yourself if you know the right questions to ask. As you work through this book of self-questions, I suggest you get a notebook or journal, and write the question on paper in longhand (not typing) which facilitates deeper thinking. Close your eyes, take a few deep, cleansing breaths, and repeat the question out loud or in your head. Then start writing what comes to your mind.

The questions are arranged by specific areas of your life. Review these different areas to see where you need the most inner work and evolution. You might want to focus on one particular area at a time, beginning with the area where you're having the most confusion or difficulty. Or you might choose to go through the entire list of questions from beginning to end as one big self-improvement makeover.

Self-Discovery Questions

Consider working on a question or two a week, writing your initial thoughts, and then coming back to the question over the subsequent days to create action steps or ideas about how to implement any changes the question invites. Some questions might compel you to meet with someone, to seek advice or counsel, or make physical changes in your environment.

Other questions might involve creating new habits, breaking old patterns, or even overhauling an entire area of your life. As you have certain insights, you might experience grief, remorse, or regret—but you also might experience elation, freedom, and surprise.

Allow yourself to feel these feelings, knowing they will pass in time. As you make positive changes based on your responses to these questions, your initial reactions will ultimately transform into contentment and inner peace.

The most valuable part of this self-coaching work is your commitment to taking the actions you create in response to the questions. Change doesn't occur in the mind—it only begins there. Change requires you to do something. Awareness often compels you to take action, but sometimes awareness is frightening, intimidating, or confusing. Sometimes we are uncomfortable with our own answers or the actions our answers require us to take.

This is where the most profound personal growth happens. When you acknowledge your fear or discomfort and then do what needs to be done anyway, you have stretched yourself, empowering you to do more to create the life you want and to become the person you know you can be. With every action you take, you'll feel more empowered and confident about initiating change in your life. You'll view these questions as the doorway to an authentic life grounded in a solid knowledge of who you are and what you desire.

Self-Awareness

1. Who am I?

This not a question you answer by saying, "I'm a lawyer" or "I'm a mom." It's a question that invites deeper responses, like here's what I value, here's what brings me joy, here's what motivates me, here's the way I want to live my life. Your answers to this may mutate over time. That's why it's important to ask this question of yourself frequently.

2. What are my top five personal and professional values?

Your core values are your guiding principles for your life and work. Defining these values gives you a touchstone for making all important decisions in your life. If you need help defining your values,

Access the words at
http://www.barriedavenport.com/list-of-400-values/.

3. How am I living outside of my values?

If you make choices in your personal or professional life that don't support your values, it's inevitable
that you'll feel unhappy and out-of-balance. Look
carefully at your life right now to see how it might
not match these important values.

4. How am I living outside of my integrity?

Your integrity is your standard of moral conduct. It's
what you believe to be right and wrong, good or
bad, healthy or unhealthy. Living outside of your
integrity creates feelings of guilt, shame, and remorse which hold you back from self-esteem and
joy. How can you reclaim your integrity so you can
feel peace of mind again?

5. What do I fear the most?

We all have fears in life, but most of our fears relate
to anxious thoughts about the future. We're afraid
of failure, illness, death, embarrassment, rejection,
and many other things. Often we have one or two

persistent fears we struggle with most often. What are yours?

6. What fears have actually come true in my life?

Have you ever noticed how most of your fears never come to pass? We might spend countless hours fretting about something that doesn't materialize. Or if it does, it isn't nearly as bad as we feared it would be. How many of your fears have actually come to pass, and were you able to manage them when they did?

7. How do my close friends and family view me?

Seeing yourself through the eyes of those closest to you gives you a great picture of many of your true attributes. Often we see ourselves quite differently from the way we are viewed by others. If you don't know how others see you, ask them. Reach out to family and friends and ask them to describe you and share how they perceive your strengths and weaknesses.

8. What are my greatest strengths?

What do you believe are your strengths of character, personality, and aptitudes? Where have you felt
the most accomplished and successful? Defining
and acknowledging your strengths will improve your
confidence and self-esteem and show you where to
focus your energies—on those areas where you
excel.

9. What are my weaknesses?

It's hard to face our weaknesses, but it's important
to do so in order to grow both personally and pro-
fessionally. We want to play to our strengths, but
also work on strengthening our weaknesses, which
builds character, patience, and self-discipline.

10. What beliefs am I holding on to that are no longer true for me?

Most of our beliefs about the world around us don't
arise from our inner selves. We adopt the beliefs of
our parents, our community, society, the media, our
peer group, our bosses, and any number of people
we associate with. Examine all of your beliefs—
political, spiritual, societal, etc.—to see where some
of these beliefs no longer reflect who you really are.

11. How am I living a lie or living inauthentically?

Acknowledging how you are holding on to old beliefs is one way of letting go of a lie. How else might you be living inauthentically? Often we pretend to be someone or something that we really aren't. Or we hold on to a deep secret or past lie that holds the key to our true selves, but we're afraid to unlock the door. Living your truth is the only way to experience happiness and peace of mind.

12. Do I have shame or guilt that needs to be resolved?

Feelings of shame and guilt can hold you back from experiencing joy in life and can impact your confidence and self-esteem. If shame and guilt are related to something that needs to be resolved, what can you do to foster resolution? Sometime shame and guilt are unfounded and result from the expectations or behaviors of others. This kind of shame requires the support of a counselor or other helping professional.

13. What am I doing to further my personal and/or spiritual growth?

Self-awareness requires ongoing inner work and continued personal and spiritual growth. This growth is facilitated by self-questioning, reflection, reading, being mentored, or participating in study groups. The more self-aware you become, the more you're able to create your life and relationships around your authentic desires and goals.

14. Do I know and understand my personality type and whether I'm an introvert or extravert?

Your personality type helps you understand more about your natural aptitudes, interests, and preferences. Knowing your type helps you recognize why you behave and think the way you do, what kind of career you're best suited to, and what personality types in others are best suited to you. Knowing whether you're an introvert or extravert helps you manage your life in a way that sustains your energy rather than depletes it. You can read more about personality type here.

See
http://liveboldandbloom.com/01/career/personality-type-how-it-impacts-3-key-areas-of-your-life

15. Do I mostly see the glass as half empty or half full?

When you think about your life circumstances, do the negative, challenging events appear in the fore-front of your thoughts, or do you focus on the positive, happy aspects of life? Be honest with yourself when answering this. Most of us dwell too much on negative thoughts, and your awareness of this can help you shift from negative to positive thinking.

16. How am I giving away my personal power?

Sometimes we unconsciously allow other people or situations to control us and make us fearful of expressing our true desires. We disempower ourselves because we don't want conflict or the discomfort of asking for what we want, especially if it will cause discord. When you give away your personal power, you chip away at your self-esteem and resign yourself to a mediocre life.

17. How am I struggling against life?

Any amount of struggle claims your energy. Often we are so dead set on a particular path or course of action that we push forward even when all of the signs tell us it's the wrong direction. Or we adamantly resist change because we are so committed to the status quo. When we release the struggle and go with the flow, often we find we have a better outcome with far less pain and energy.

18. What are the most important life lessons I've learned so far?

Simply by living we learn invaluable lessons. Most often, it's the challenges and difficulties of life that teach us the greatest lessons. Sometimes we resist looking back at past challenges because it's painful, but it's important to reflect on what you learned from these situations in order to use this knowledge for future endeavors and personal growth.

19. How am I unnecessarily complicating my life?

All of us tend to make our lives more complicated than they need to be. We do this by filling our schedules with too many obligations and unnecessary tasks. We also complicate our lives with unhealthy relationships, jobs we don't like, and more material things than we really need. All of these complications distract us from what is truly important and meaningful to us.

20. What do I believe gives meaning and purpose to my life?

Once you define what is meaningful and provides purpose to your life, you'll find it's far easier to rid yourself of complications and distractions. When you have a purpose, you are focused and determined in a joyful way. You no longer have time for "filler" activities and superficial interests.

Potential

21. If I had unlimited financial resources, where and how would I live?

We tend to believe a lack of money holds us back from our dreams, but if you had all the money you need, what would be your dream life? Often when we take the time to define our dream life and write it down, it becomes more real and achievable in our minds. Write down what your life would be like if you had unlimited resources.

22. What do I feel passionate about?

Passions are those activities you "can't not do." They are the endeavors that draw us in and keep us focused, excited, and engaged. These endeavors can be in your professional and personal life. They might be hobbies, a cause you feel strongly about, or a business you find compelling. If you don't know what you're passionate about, take the time to find out. You can begin by taking this passion quiz at http://pathtopassioncourse.com/.

23. What is my vision for my life for the next ten years?

Creating a planned vision for your life gives you a roadmap to make your goals and passions come to life. You can allow life to just happen as it may with you as a reactor, or you can be a creator of your life, envisioning your future while remaining open to all possibilities.

24. What specific actions am I taking to make that vision a reality?

Your vision can't manifest on its own. You have to make it happen. It happens by outlining the specific, small daily actions you need to take to move forward toward that vision. Are you acting on your vision or just dreaming about it? Only action determines your reality.

25. On a scale of 1–10, with 10 being the highest, how would I rate my quality of life right now?

Where are you right now in your dreams for a better you and a better life? Are you living a great life and want to make it even better? Or do you feel very little about your life is working? Look at every area of your life, from your career to your relationships, and decide where you need to buff up your actions and choices. What can you do right now to raise your standards?

26. If I scored 6 or below, what specifically is hindering my quality of life?

Often we live with less in our lives because something holds us back from claiming the life we really want. Sometimes it's low self-esteem. Often it's fear of change or risk. Other times we don't make positive changes in our own lives for fear of making someone else upset. How are you holding yourself back from a high quality of life and making the changes necessary to live up to your own standards?

27. What goal or dream have I given up on and why?

Have you had a goal or dream in the past that really excited you, but you let it go or never followed through? If so, what got in your way or undermined your enthusiasm or motivation? Is that roadblock still relevant or real? Is it time to revisit this goal or dream?

28. What skills or aptitudes am I allowing to lie dormant?

We are all born with aptitudes for a variety of skills. We develop and refine some of these aptitudes, but others never see the light of day. They remain dormant within us, just waiting to be explored, practiced, and mastered. Until we explore these areas, we don't know how they might positively impact our lives and future success and happiness.

29. What would I most like to change about my life?

What is the low-hanging fruit in your life that begs for change and attention? Maybe it's a relationship problem or the need for a job change. Maybe you aren't taking care of your health and fitness, or you don't feel you are surrounded by the right people. What is the one change you could make that would positively impact all other areas of your life?

30. What are the first five steps in making that change?

There's nothing holding you back from starting the process of making that life change. You might be filled with doubts and excuses, but those are almost always just negative voices in your head. What five actions can you take right away to get the ball rolling? Beginning is always the hardest part of change.

31. What am I doing to continue to improve myself, my skills, and my overall expertise?

A fulfilling life requires lifelong learning and growth. The more you learn, the more skills and experiences you have, the more marketable you'll be in your career—and the more interesting person you'll be in general. What actions are you taking to continue learning and skill-building?

Life Priorities

32. What is my most urgent personal and professional problem or challenge?

Life constantly presents us with challenges and difficulties. They arise in our personal and professional lives. We'd much prefer to push these aside or deal with them later, but right now is the best time to deal with the issue at hand. Define the most pressing problems you are facing right now.

33. What am I doing to handle these problems?

Now that you've acknowledged these issues, what specific actions can you take to resolve them? Even though it may be uncomfortable to deal with these problems, the longer you allow them to go unaddressed, the more energy and motivation they drain from you.

34. What commitments or projects am I spending time on that really aren't my priorities?

Life often has a way of running us rather than the other way around. People make demands of us, or we feel obligated to give our time away to something or someone that's really not a priority for us. How are you giving away your time rather than spending it on what is truly important and meaningful for you?

35. Where do I feel the most overwhelmed or stressed?

When you fill your life with unnecessary commitments and obligations, often your body and emotions will tell you that your priorities are out of balance. Pay attention to your stress level and your feelings of anxiety, irritation, or frustration. What is the source of these feelings?

36. What specific actions can I take to reduce the overwhelm and stress?

Once you've identified the feelings and the cause of the feelings, you can take action to eliminate or at least reduce the source of your stress. Often we believe we have no alternatives to relieve ourselves of these stressful situations, but there is always another way. What actions can you take in the next few days to reduce your stress?

37. What opportunities do I have available to me that I'm not taking advantage of?

You might be missing opportunities or priorities right in front of you that you simply haven't pursued. Maybe there are people in your life who could support you, or skills you possess that you haven't fully taken advantage of. Think carefully about the opportunities you might be missing in your own life.

38. How will I feel if I let these opportunities pass me by?

When you recognize these opportunities, you might see how your life could be better, happier, and richer if you pursued them. This might take some effort, but if you miss these opportunities because of inertia or distraction, how will you feel later? Will you regret allowing them to pass you by?

39. What do I need to do to take advantage of these opportunities?

How can you get the ball rolling to seize an opportunity that's available to you? What are two or three actions you can take to make this a priority in your life right now?

40. How are my current life or work priorities out of alignment with my core values?

When you are living out of alignment with your core values, you will feel off balance and inauthentic. You might even feel some guilt or uneasiness about how you're spending your time. Revisit your core values to see where you might not be honoring them in your daily priorities.

41. What do I need to do to realign my life or work with my values?

If you see that some aspect of your life or work isn't aligned with your values, what needs to change to correct that? You might need to talk this through with a coach, friend, or counselor to develop a strategy for transitioning to something different.

42. Do I have a legacy I want to leave for the world, and if so, what is it?

Your long term priorities should reflect bigger goals and a more profound purpose for your life. What do you believe your purpose is for your life? How do you want to impact your family, community, and the world? What specific actions are you taking to create your legacy?

Career

43. What five things do I spend most of my work day focused on?

We tend to be creatures of habit, even in our work. We have patterns of checking emails, allowing for interruptions, and creating other distractions that pull us from the valuable work that needs to be done. The way you spend your work days impacts your level of success in your career.

44. Are these five things aligned with my career values and my weekly, monthly, and annual goals?

Be honest with yourself about how you spend your time. You have career goals and values which should determine your daily activities and tasks. Are you highly focused on these important activities, or are you spending too much time doing things that don't further your goals or support your values?

45. If not, what do I need to change in order to shift my focus and daily work priorities?

How can you shift your daily actions to be more focused on what truly matters and what makes a difference in your career trajectory or the bottom line of your business? What bad habits or unconscious behaviors are you willing to change to move the needle closer to your goals?

46. How much more money could I make if I were more focused and were properly inspired and supported?

Consider if you spent just 10 percent more time each day doing the valuable work that produces income or gets the attention of decision makers at your office? Or if you had the resources and support you need? How would that potentially impact your income?

47. On a scale of 1–10, with 10 being the highest, how passionate do I feel about my job?

When you are passionate about your profession, it doesn't feel like work. It feels exciting and fulfilling. An uninspired, boring, passionless job depletes your energy and demotivates you. Where does your job fall on the passion scale?

48. What needs to change in order to feel more passionate about my work?

How can you be more passionate in the career you are in—or what do you need to do to find a job that makes you feel passionate? What are some specific actions you can take to find your true calling?

49. Where is the stress coming from in my work?

If you are feeling stressed, overwhelmed, and unhappy with your job, take the time to think about the source of your feelings. Sometimes we carry low-level feelings of stress and anxiety that seep out in the way we interact with others or in our health, but we may not be consciously aware of why we're feeling this way. Examine your feelings to get to the root cause

50. How can I reduce or eliminate this stress?

Once you identify the source of your work-related stress, brainstorm ways you can address the stress and diminish or eliminate it. What specific actions can you take to start the process? For some ideas to help you relieve stress, go to this site: http://liveboldandbloom.com/12/self-improvement/feeling-stressed-out-10-ways-to-relieve-stress

51. What conflicts am I having at work?

It's possible some of your stress is related to con-flicts with your work associates, your boss, or your clients. Are you aware of any ongoing conflicts or simmering tensions? Do you feel uncomfortable or ill-at-ease with anyone you work with?

52. What role do I play in these conflicts and what do I need to change?

If you do have direct conflict or tension with some-one, examine your own role in the issue. It is much easier to change our own behaviors first, rather than hoping to change another person. Be honest with yourself about your contribution to the problem and how you need to change.

53. What are the most and least fulfilling aspects of my work?

Have you taken the time to look at what you really enjoy about your job? Even the smallest perks can add to your happiness and fulfillment on the job. Also examine what you don't enjoy about your job and why you don't enjoy it. Knowing what you do and don't like will help you when and if you change jobs. It can also help you focus more on the parts of your job you do like.

54. Am I working with the right people? The best people?

One of the most important factors in career happiness is the people you're surrounded by. Are you inspired, motivated, and challenged by the people around you? Are they highly-motivated, energetic, and passionate? Are they lifting you up or dragging you down?

55. What strengths and skills do I possess that are immediately marketable?

If you needed to leave your current job today, do you have the necessary skills to find another position quickly? Are you aware of your strengths and weaknesses and what your boss perceives those to be? What do you need to do to make yourself more marketable and appealing to future employers?

56. What resources am I missing that are necessary for my career success?

Do you have a vision for your career? Where do you hope to be in the next five to ten years? If you know your vision, how do you intend to get there and what resources, do you need to make it happen?

57. How can I go about getting those resources?

If you need extra skills, training, education, access to information or tools, where can you find those resources and how can you gain access to them? What is your plan for taking advantage of the necessary resources in order to reach your goals?

58. What are five specific actions I can take to improve my career situation?

If you feel overwhelmed by the changes you need to make in your career to move forward or find something you feel passionate about, simply begin with the first five actions. What are the best, most obvious actions you can take to improve your situation?

Finances

59. On a scale of 1–10, with 10 being very secure and well-managed, how secure and well-managed is my financial situation?

Many people don't take the time to gain a clear picture of their finances. As a result, they overspend, get in debt, or neglect to manage their money to make it work for them. How well are you managing your money?

60. How stable is my income stream?

Can you count on a regular monthly income with a solid amount of job security? If your income isn't predictable and you don't have job security, do you feel comfortable with this uncertainty and risk?

61. Do I live within, below, or beyond my means?

Living beyond your means will create a huge burden of debt over time. Living below your means allows you to save for emergencies and big expenses. What can you do to begin living below your means? How much are you willing to put aside, and how will this change your lifestyle?

62. Do I have an emergency fund or savings put aside that would pay my bills for at least six months?

By living below your means, especially if your job or income is unpredictable, you are creating a safety net of savings that can see you through the times when your income isn't coming in or your job goes away. What do you need to do to build up six months' worth of savings?

63. How much credit card debt do I have, and what is my plan for reducing the debt?

Allowing credit card debt to accumulate is a slippery slope. It's easy to hand over the credit card when you are longing for that new dress or the latest gadget. But credit card debt adds up quickly with steep interest fees and late payments. Try to avoid using credit cards as much as possible, and pay with cash instead.

64. How much money is enough for me?

Take the time to think about how much money is really enough for you. At some point, there's a diminishing point of return when it comes to income and life satisfaction. The more you make, the more complicated and demanding your life becomes. Create your own bottom line when it comes to a satisfactory income.

65. What are my financial goals?

When you define how much money is enough, then it's time to figure out how you're going to get there. What financial milestones do you need to create in order to live the way you want to live?

66. What plans do I have in place to reach those goals?

Once you've defined your financial goals, then you need to get granular with your actions. Do you need to cut back on expenses? Pay off debt? Find a way

to make more money? Research the best invest-
ments and retirement plans? You can't reach your
financial goals without creating and implementing
your strategy.

67. What mistakes do I tend to make with money?

Most of us have made some poor decisions about
money in the past. We've been through phases of
overspending, getting into debt, or neglecting to
save. What is your Achilles heel when it comes to
money? What do you need to do to turn that
around?

68. What holds me back financially?

Do you have a mental or career roadblock standing
in your way of reaching your financial goals? Do
you have limiting beliefs about your ability to make
money or hold on to it? Be honest with yourself and
pinpoint what might be blocking you from being fi-
nancially successful and secure.

69. What is my mental attitude about money— do I see it as a plentiful or scarce resource?

Often we have attitudes about money that were handed down to us from our parents. If our parents had a "lack mentality," we might see money as a scarce resource, with only so much to go around. This attitude makes us fearful and tight with our money. Do you see money as a very limited resource or one that is readily available to you? How is your attitude impacting your financial success?

Confidence and Self-Esteem

70. Where do I feel the most confident?

We can feel confident in some areas of our lives but not in others. We might feel great about our relationship skills, but we have self-doubt about our ability to succeed in business. Or we might be terribly shy in social settings, but completely confident working on a project. In what parts of your life do you feel the most confident?

71. Why do I feel confident in these areas?

Think back to the events and circumstances that allowed you to feel confident in these areas. Do you feel more skilled or more naturally accomplished? Have others reinforced you? Try to figure out the path to your confidence in these areas and how it might be applied to some low confidence parts of your life.

72. Where do I feel the least confident?

Follow the same exercise, examining your life for the areas where you're lacking confidence.

73. Why am I lacking confidence in these areas?

Again, consider the events and circumstances leading to your low confidence. Keep digging until you feel you've found the root cause. More than likely, the original cause is no longer relevant or true.

74. Where do I most want to improve my confidence?

There are some low-confidence areas that impact all other parts of our lives. If you lack confidence in social settings for example, it undermines your success at work, with friendships, and with your love relationships. By improving one area, you boost your confidence in many areas. What is the low-hanging confidence fruit that needs the most attention in your life?

75. What has been holding me back from improving my confidence?

Sometimes we simply accept low confidence because we don't know it's possible to improve it. Or we may feel so uncomfortable, we don't want to draw any more attention to our self-doubts and insecurities. What has prevented you from working on your confidence?

76. What do I believe about myself that I know isn't true?

One of the main issues keeping us from improving confidence is limiting beliefs. Perhaps we were shamed or criticized in our youth, and we continue to hold these beliefs about ourselves. Or maybe a past failure or mistake leads us to believe we will never be successful. What beliefs are you hanging on to that are no longer true?

77. What do I believe about myself that is true?

Perhaps there are areas of your life that need improvement, and this is undermining your confidence. We might lack skill, training, or experience which makes us feel inadequate. What limiting beliefs hold some truth and need your attention in order to boost your confidence?

78. Do I like and love myself?

A big part of confidence is having the foundation of self-esteem. Self-esteem requires you to accept yourself as you are, while having the emotional maturity to recognize where you need to improve. It requires that you like the person you see in the mirror, and that you have enough love for that person that you can show compassion and forgiveness when necessary.

79. What don't I like about myself?

If you don't like yourself, what exactly is it that you don't like? Is this something you can change or improve? If so, list the steps you need to take to make those changes. If not, can you begin to recognize the healing power of self-acceptance and acknowledge that everyone has flaws?

80. How do other people perceive me?

Often our self-perceptions differ greatly from the perceptions of others. How do you think your close friends, family, and work associates view you? How would they describe your strengths and weaknesses? If you don't know, ask them to give you real feedback.

81. What were my parents' expectations of me growing up?

Did you have parents who were highly critical, demanding, or demeaning? Or were your parents supportive, encouraging, and positive? Did they allow you to make mistakes and learn from experience, or did they step in and rescue you whenever you encountered a problem? Often our parents' expectations and behaviors around our successes and failures can have a huge impact on our levels of confidence.

82. How did their expectations impact my self-esteem and confidence?

As you think back on your parents' expectations of you and how they handled those expectations, consider how their behavior and words impacted the way you feel about yourself and your abilities. If they undermined your self-esteem and confidence, can you identify where their words and expectations are no longer true for your adult self?

83. What events growing up negatively impacted my self-esteem and confidence?

Our parents aren't the only influence on how we view ourselves. Peers, teachers, role models, and many others can impact us. Even small events from the past can stick with us for years, making us feel inadequate and insecure. Can you identify any of these situations you're still hanging on to?

84. How am I still holding on to those negative events?

Think about the specific ways these past events and people are still impacting you today. How are you holding yourself back or putting yourself down as a result of these situations?

85. What events in my adult life have undermined my self-esteem and confidence?

It's not just your past life that contributes to low confidence and self-esteem. Any number of adult experiences can knock us flat and sabotage our inner strength. It can take years to recover our confidence after the loss of a job, a divorce, or a financial disaster.

86. What did I learn from those events?

Even the most difficult life events, the ones that wipe out our confidence and smash our self-esteem, are packed with life lessons if we look for them. What have you learned from these experiences that you can use to rebuild your confidence?

87. What skills am I not utilizing that would improve my confidence?

We often have skills we take for granted or don't fully recognize. These skills can be applied to your career, your relationships, or any other endeavor that might improve your level of confidence. Examine your own skills to see how you might be ignoring some that could be useful and valuable.

88. What skills do I need to learn that would improve my confidence?

Sometimes the only thing standing between you and your confidence is feeling you have the necessary skills, proper training, or enough knowledge and experience to perform successfully. What skills or training would help you boost your confidence?

89. What emotions do I feel when faced with situations that make me lose my confidence?

Low confidence can make us anxious, guilty, embarrassed, angry, and frustrated. These emotions add a second layer of difficulty to our lack of confidence. This further depletes our energy and motivation and makes it more difficult to work on building our confidence.

90. How can I make these emotions less powerful?

When you want to build your confidence, begin by addressing the emotions low confidence fosters. Acknowledge that in spite of your lack of confidence, you are a worthy and valuable person. You do have what it takes to improve your confidence, even if your emotions make you feel otherwise. Talk to a friend, coach, or counselor about your feelings to help you work through them.

91. Am I willing to live with some emotional discomfort in order to improve my self-esteem and confidence?

Any positive change requires you to challenge and stretch yourself. In order to improve confidence and self-esteem, you have to challenge yourself to take actions which make you uncomfortable or anxious. But when you successfully follow through, you'll see how your confidence improves.

92. What confident actions would feel like a do-able stretch challenge for me?

One of the best ways to improve your confidence is by taking small actions in the area where you lack confidence. If you lack confidence meeting new people, make a point of introducing yourself to people you encounter in daily life. Get accustomed to the discomfort of challenging yourself, and over time your confidence will grow and it will get easier.

93. What do I need to improve about myself or my circumstances to maximize my chances for success?

If you lack confidence about your appearance, what can you do to improve your appearance? If you lack confidence about speaking in public, how can you become more skilled speaking? If you feel shy with meeting a potential romantic partner, how can you open up more? View your low confidence as a problem to be solved. What is the first step you need to take?

Life Problems

94. What problems and crises do I keep attracting in my life?

Problems and crises that recur in your life are good signs of where you need the most awareness and growth. These problems can reflect our insecurities, blind spots, or emotionally immature behaviors. Consistently choosing unsupportive, controlling, or emotionally unavailable people suggests a self-esteem issue.

95. What is my role in these problems?

As you become aware of the problems and crises that recur, think about how your behaviors, decisions, and words might contribute to these problems. What can you change about yourself and your interactions with others that might prevent some of these issues from occurring again.

96. What do I keep doing that limits my success?

Sometimes we are afraid of success, or we believe we don't deserve success. Or we might unknowingly behave in ways or make decisions that keep us from success. How are you holding yourself back from success, and what are you willing to change to correct that?

97. How am I fooling myself or others by pretending or ignoring a situation?

Life can get uncomfortable and intimidating at times—so much so that we bury our heads in the sand or pretend that everything is OK when it's not. How are you fooling yourself or pretending in front of others?

98. Is there a common theme I see with my past failures and mistakes, and if so, what is it?

Think about the mistakes you've made or the failures you've experienced in the past. Do you see a common thread running through these situations? It could be a behavior, a decision-making process, a lack of planning, or an experience. By seeking out the common theme from the past, you can save yourself from making the same mistakes in the future.

99. How much time do I spend thinking about the past or worrying about the future?

The only reality is the present moment, yet most of our thoughts relate to something that's already happened or something yet to happen. How much of your life are you relinquishing to negative thinking, worry, or regret?

100. What coping skills do I use to handle life difficulties and failures?

When you do experience problems and disappointments in life, what do you do to manage your feelings and move forward with your life? If you don't having coping skills at your disposal, this is the time to create some. These might include a supportive network of friends and family, a coach or counselor, prayer or meditation, or exercise.

101. Am I experiencing any emotional difficulties that I'm not addressing?

Think about how you've been feeling for the last few weeks. Have you felt anxious, depressed, angry, sad, stressed, or irritable? Maybe you've felt these emotions but haven't paid much attention to them. You can't leave them unchecked, so take some time to identify the cause of your emotions.

102. If so, what do I need to do to address these difficulties?

Once you've identified your emotions and what's triggered them, think about how you can address the trigger and the feelings. If you remove or diminish whatever caused you to feel bad, then do so. If not, go back to your coping skills and find a way to work through the negative emotions.

103. Do I have a fundamental lie or deeply guarded secret that is causing guilt, shame, fear, or depression?

Some of our most negative, debilitating feelings come from holding on to a lie or secret. Ongoing guilt and shame can eat away at you and demolish your peace of mind and self-esteem. Find a professional counselor or someone you trust and come clean. The relief you feel will be liberating, and quite often it's not nearly as bad or shameful as you feared.

104. How well do I recover from disappointments and failure?

The most successful, confident people are able to quickly move past failure and disappointments without letting these issues drag them down or hold them back from their next endeavor. If failure debilitates you for months, or you find yourself dwelling on it every time you try something new, you need a strategy for moving past failure and learning from it. Look at your past disappointments and failures, and write down the lessons you have learned that you can use for the future.

105. What kind of support or resources do I need to correct any life problems or difficulties I'm experiencing right now?

If you are going through a difficulty or problem right now, you may be neglecting to find the support and resources you need to help you through it. Think carefully about what would help ease you through this situation. Reach out to friends and family. Practice compassionate self care. Don't neglect yourself during this time when you most need support.

Health

106. What are my feelings about my body?

Your body image can impact your confidence, health, and relationships. When you don't respect your body, or if you have negative feelings about your body, you're more likely to mistreat it and not take care of your health. If you can make healthy changes to improve your body image, what actions can you take? If you can't change your body, begin to practice acceptance and love for your body in spite of its flaws.

107. What are my feelings about aging?

Do you fear aging or see it as a time of decline and loss? Or do you look forward to continued experiences, growth, and joy as you get older? Your attitude toward aging impacts your mental and physical health. What can you do to improve your attitude about getting older?

108. How do my feelings about my body and aging impact my health decisions?

If you have a desire to remain healthy, fit, and active as you get older, then you'll be more motivated to take care of yourself. You'll stay on top of preventative healthcare appointments and design your diet and fitness so you can enjoy optimum health. What health decisions are you making that either support or undermine your health and body image?

109. Am I at a healthy weight for my height?

Being overweight has serious health consequences that impact your quality of life and longevity. Have you allowed extra weight to creep up on you? Are you making excuses for those few extra pounds or have you stopped caring about your weight? Review the healthy weight requirements for your height and age to be sure you know the recommended weight for you. Access http://www.calculator.net/ideal-weight-calculator.html.

110. Do I get regular, aerobic exercise at least five days a week for at least 30 minutes a day, as well as muscle strengthening exercise at least twice a week?

Whether or not you are overweight, you need two types of physical activity each week for optimal health. The health benefits of regular exercise are hard to ignore. If you are skipping out on exercise, ask yourself why. Why do you not respect your body enough to take care of it appropriately? What small steps can you take to begin a daily exercise program?

111. Is my diet heavy in fresh vegetables and fruits, as well as lean meat (for meat eaters) and whole grains?

There is plenty of accessible information online and in other media about foods that are healthy and unhealthy. You know that a plant-heavy diet with lean meats, whole grains, little sugar, and non-processed foods is the best for your body. Are you ready to respect your body and treat it well by feeding it healthy foods?

112. What do I need to change about my diet and fitness habits?

In general, what bad habits do you have related to diet and exercise that are holding you back from optimal health? Be real with yourself and honest about how you might be harming your health and impacting your longevity. Are you really willing to change?

113. Do I get regularly scheduled physicals and exams and recommended preventative procedures?

Not only do exercise and diet impact your health, but also your commitment to preventative healthcare makes a difference in your quality of life and longevity. What check-ups or procedures are you putting off or ignoring? What could be the consequences of not handling these important appointments?

114. Do I have strategies for managing stress?

Stress is a silent thief of your physical and mental well-being. Chronic stress can have serious health implications. Pay attention to the sources of your stress or the triggers that ignite anxiety and tension.

What strategies do you have ready when stress overwhelms you? Do you utilize stress reduction techniques rather than ignoring your stress?

115. If I don't take care of my health, what is this telling me about my beliefs about myself, or what does it reveal about me?

When you don't take care of yourself by ignoring your health, avoiding exercise, and eating poorly, you reveal a lack of self-care and self-compassion. What excuses are you making that hide deeper feelings of low self-esteem, fear, or denial? What false beliefs do you hold to make you feel it's OK to ignore your health?

116. What habits do I have that are not good for my mental or physical health?

Do you have other bad habits—like smoking, drinking too much, or taking drugs—that compromise your health and wellbeing? Do you have a serious addiction that you're not facing, or even a minor addiction you pretend is really nothing? Can you be honest with yourself and your loved ones that you are making destructive choices?

117. What can I do to change those habits?

Once you have full awareness around your self-destructive habits, it's hard to just continue on as though everything is just fine. Change is now the only course of action. What is the first step you need to take to release these bad habits? Are you willing to take that first step today?

Relationships

118. Am I generally happy in my primary love relationship?

Is your marriage or love relationship a source of joy and fulfillment, or is there constant conflict, a lack of intimacy, and poor communication? What is the truth of your relationship? Is it more good than bad or more bad than good? Only complete honesty will allow you to heal and correct any issues.

119. If I'm not happy, what is the reason for my unhappiness?

Can you pinpoint the main cause of your unhappiness or dissatisfaction in your relationship? Is there a particular trigger for conflict or loss of connection? Do both of you feel unhappy or just you?

120. What role do I play in my relationship un-happiness?

When we're unhappy in our marriage or partner-ship, we tend to want to blame the other person. They haven't supported us. They don't make us happy. They push us away. Before you begin blam-ing, look closely at yourself first. What part do you play in the difficulties you have? How are your be-haviors, words, and actions contributing to or exac-erbating disconnection and pain?

121. What do I need to do specifically to im-prove my love relationship?

The only person you have the power to change in this relationship is yourself. You might ask for change from your partner, but you can't require it. You can change the way you respond to the prob-lems. You can put the health of the relationship be-fore your own needs or feelings. You can ask for relationship counseling or coaching. Think of spe-cific ways you can improve yourself and the situa-tion.

122. What complaints have I consistently heard in my current and past relationships that I need to work on?

Sometimes we aren't aware of how we contribute to relationship problems. We are blind to our own insecurities, knee-jerk reactions, and unkindnesses. Look back over relationships you've had in the past. Do you see a consistent pattern of complaints from your past partners or love interests about your behavior? Pay attention to these patterns and see them as important areas of growth for you.

123. What valuable lessons have I learned from past or current relationships?

Our intimate relationships provide us a wellspring of opportunities for learning and growth that we can take on to the next relationship. Relationships bring out the best and worst in us and reflect back to us our deepest fears and longings. Think about every important love relationship you've ever had. What lessons, both good and bad, did you learn from each person?

124. How am I compromising myself in my love relationship or in any relationship?

A healthy relationship allows you to become more of yourself, rather than forcing you to diminish yourself. It requires a reasonable amount of self-esteem and confidence from both people so that the relationship is grounded in mutual respect and intimacy. When you give up part of yourself to please someone out of fear or insecurity, you create imbalance and undermine the authenticity of the connection.

125. What am I tolerating that I don't want to tolerate in any relationship?

Compromising yourself often involves tolerating words, behavior, or decisions you don't want or like. Tolerating creates resentments, anger, and frustration that sucks the joy out of the connection. Where do you feel resentment or anger over something you are tolerating in your relationships?

126. What boundaries do I need to set to stop tolerating these things?

Sometimes we let things go on and tolerate them because we don't want to make waves, or we fear rejection. In healthy relationships, you have the freedom to kindly express your boundaries and request behavior change. Creating boundaries might be uncomfortable and create temporary discord, but ultimately the other person will respect you more.

127. How well do I manage conflict in my relationships, and what do I need to do to improve?

Conflict is inevitable in your love relationship. But how you handle conflict can make or break the relationship. Unkind words, passive aggressive actions, threats, and stonewalling are emotionally immature behaviors that push a couple further and further apart. When conflicts arise, what do you do to resolve the conflict in a way that puts the health of the relationship first?

128. Am I getting my most important needs met in my relationship?

Everyone has needs they want met in their love relationships. These needs can include affection, intimacy, quality time, emotional support, and sexual connection. Your partner may not know all of your primary relationship needs. If some of your needs aren't being met, how can you communicate them to your partner to ask for what you desire?

129. Am I honoring the important needs of my love partner, children, friends, and family?

Your love partner and the people in other close relationships also have needs. It's likely you aren't meeting all of their needs, as we can't be all things to all people. But you can show love and attention to these people by asking them what their needs are and how you can help meet them.

130. Do I use passive aggressive behavior or manipulation to get my needs met?

When we expect our partner to read our minds and meet our needs without telling them what we desire, then we set them up for failure. Often we resort to back-handed words and actions to try to get our needs met. How are you failing to be direct and open with your partner? What behaviors do you need to stop that are passive or manipulative?

131. Have I left anything unresolved with someone I care about?

It's nearly impossible to have intimacy and connection in any relationship when there's an unresolved conflict or unspoken issue between you. What is the elephant in the room with any of your relationships? Are you harboring anger, guilt, or resentment— or do you think someone has these feelings about you?

132. If so, what do I need to do to resolve it?

What specific steps do you need to take to resolve any issues or lingering negative feelings between you and someone you care about? Are you willing to say something, even if it's uncomfortable, to break the ice and repair the relationship? Is the relationship worth this discomfort to you?

133. Am I able to apologize completely and freely when I've done something wrong?

Can you easily recognize when you've said or done something wrong or hurtful? Can you take full responsibility for your actions and admit your mistake? Do you show remorse and offer an unconditional apology?

134. Do I need to apologize to anyone?

Is there anyone in your life right now to whom you need to apologize? Or is there anyone from your past you neglected to apologize to who should hear your apology now? What are you willing to do this week to set things right?

135. Do I offer forgiveness freely and completely?

An apology isn't genuine unless it's offered freely and without conditions or excuses. You must completely own your mistake and do what you can to rectify the situation. The only way to regain trust and restore the situation fully is by not repeating the behavior or words that required the apology.

136. How am I attempting to control or change someone else?

Sometimes we try to bend others to our will or desires through manipulation, passive aggressive behaviors, or intimidation. We want things to go our way, and we want others to recognize that our way is the best way. When our egos get in the way, we see the people around us as extensions of ourselves, so we try to change them to reflect well on us. We don't fully accept them for who and what they are.

137. How am I isolating myself or pushing others away?

Do you find yourself spending a lot of time alone, avoiding social events, or even sabotaging relationships to push people away? This could be a sign of low self-esteem, depression, or social anxiety. Or maybe you've been wounded or rejected by someone and don't want to risk that pain again. What can you do to begin reconnecting with people?

138. Am I doing what is necessary to nurture my close relationships?

All close relationships require time and attention. They require open communication, shared experiences, and mutual respect and support. Even friends who live far away need to connect with you by phone or email regularly. Are you paying proper attention to the people you care about?

139. If not, what specific actions do I need to take?

How can you begin to appreciate and cherish the people close to you? What can you do to strengthen the connection and cultivate closeness and trust? Think of the person or people in your life whom you might be taking for granted, and consider how you would feel if they were suddenly no longer in your life. Use those feelings to motivate you to nurture these relationships.

140. Do I generally invite high quality, trustworthy people into my life? If not, why not?

Look carefully at the people you surround yourself with. Do they uplift and support you or diminish you in some way? Do they energize you or drain you? Do they have integrity and emotional maturity? Are you inspired by them or embarrassed by them? The people around you are a reflection of you. What relationships do you need to change, and how can you create a higher standard for who you select to be in your life?

Lifestyle

141. Am I living in a city and community that I love?

Your environment sets the tone for your lifestyle, and it should reflect the person you are, your interests, values, and personality. Are you living in a city or community that feels like the best fit for who you are?

142. If not, what can I do to change this?

If you don't feel you're in the right place, and that your quality of life is compromised because of where you live, are you willing to continue living this way? It may be complicated to move, but what plans can you initiate to get the ball rolling so you can live in a place that truly feels like home to you?

143. How much time do I spend every day doing things I really enjoy?

Mentally review how you spend the hours of your day. Go through each activity, and ask yourself if you feel happy or fulfilled doing what you're doing. How much time do you give up to activities that bore you or you don't like? What are you willing to do about it?

144. Am I living in a home that reflects who I am and how I want to feel?

Does your house reflect who you are, your style, and the way you want to live? Is it cluttered and untidy? Have you allowed things to look tired and dated? How do you feel when you walk in the door—restored and peaceful or stressed?

145. What do I need to do to change my home environment?

Look around your house, especially at the rooms where you spend the most time. What really bothers you about those spaces? What would you like to do to freshen up and energize the rooms? Even though you might be OK with clutter, it actually lowers your energy and creates a subtle level of anxie-ty.

146. How much time do I allow myself for brain-storming and contemplation?

Everyone needs to simply be. We need to step away from obligations, work, and distractions and quietly contemplate ourselves, our lives, and our relationships. We need the mental and physical space to allow ideas to form and creativity to flour-ish. How can you create that time for yourself?

147. Do I pay attention to my inner needs and happiness?

During this contemplation time, reflect on what you might need in your life to contribute to your happi-ness. Do you listen to your intuition and pay atten-tion to restlessness, agitation, and longing? Do you actively try to put yourself in situations where you feel happy and peaceful?

148. Do I have a fulfilling social network of friends?

Socializing with close friends is an essential element of a happy life. We all need a social network for camaraderie, support, and fun. Do you have an adequate network of friends to meet your social needs? Are these people in your "tribe"—are they likeminded, uplifting people you enjoy?

149. How do I need to simplify my lifestyle?

How complicated is your life? How many obligations and tasks have you crammed into your day? How many material things do you have that require ongoing maintenance and attention? A simple lifestyle leaves more room for relationships, experiences, and peace of mind. How can you simplify your life?

150. What could I delegate or eliminate from my life to make it more enjoyable?

If your life is complicated and over-scheduled, and you feel you don't have any time to enjoy what is meaningful and important to you, how can you carve out more time for yourself? What could you have others do for you, and what can you simply drop from your life to free up more time and space?

151. What is preventing me from living peacefully?

Do you enjoy peace of mind and freedom from worry most of the time? If not, what is holding you back from a peaceful existence? How can you create more peace and joy in your life? What needs to change?

152. Does my lifestyle reflect my core values? If not, what needs to change?

Go back and review your core values. Do your environment, home, social network, hobbies, and daily activities reflect these values? If you spend hours a day surfing the net or watching mindless television, is that aligned with your value system? Be honest with yourself, and begin to make changes in your life to match your values.

153. Do I feel fully satisfied in my lifestyle, and if not, what do I need to do about it?

Even though you might have a great lifestyle that's aligned with your values, is there something that could be better? Is there something you'd want to add to your life or change in order to make it more fulfilling and satisfying?

154. Am I living my own life or someone else's?

Does the way you live really reflect who you are, or are you living the idea of who you are supposed to be? Does something feel "off" about your life, like you're not being authentic, or you're pretending based on expectations or confusion about yourself and your place in the world? What is the first step toward living authentically and expressing your true self?

155. How do I anticipate my lifestyle will change in the next ten years?

What are your goals for how you want to live in the next ten years? Do you see yourself living in the same city or the same house? Do you envision you'll travel more or spend less time working? Do you hope to retire early or begin a family? How are you laying the groundwork for your vision of the future? What steps do you need to take in the next weeks and months?

Conclusion

The goal of these questions is to foster self-awareness and motivate you to take action for positive change. Self-inquiry puts you in complete control of your own success and personal evolution. If practiced regularly, it will eventually become an automatic response to challenges in your life and in preparing for goals you want to achieve.

Self-questioning also leads you to become more introspective and to recognize what you are feeling.

Self-questioning simply means paying attention to yourself. You pay attention to . . .

- what you are thinking
- what you are speaking
- how you are acting
- how you are feeling

- what you are eating

- what you believe

- how you are reacting

- what (and who) you are attracting

- how you make decisions

- what you are hiding

- what patterns you are seeing in your life

- how your body is responding

When you pay attention and question yourself, you are consciously tuning in. You are proactively viewing yourself from the position of your higher self—your inner personal coach—and when your higher self observes your thoughts, feelings, decisions, and actions, you are forced to discover an answer, make a decision, or take action.

As the questioner, you are compelled to recognize whether or not the answer you come up with aligns with the person you want to be. Does it align with your integrity, your values, your purpose, your passion, your spirituality, with the core of who you are?

Maybe you don't know who you are or who you wish to be because you haven't ever defined the best version of yourself. Even so, you likely have an intuition about whether your choices, beliefs, and actions are either positive or negative, life-affirming or life-destroying, peaceful or agitating. Paying attention is a call to action, and acting on a call from your higher consciousness is the path to self-awareness and a turning point in your personal evolution. You see where you are not fully yourself, and you decide to change it.

So why do you really need to ask yourself these powerful questions? From my casual observation of people, it appears most of us long for self-awareness but not many can identify the longing, and questioning creates more clarity and direction. For those of us who actively seek self-awareness, paying attention and being the questioner is a direct route to achieving what we want in life.

Paying attention requires that we . . .

- simplify our lives;

- remove distractions;

- focus on the present moment;

- train our "monkey minds" to observe rather than race;

- let go of our "ego self;"

- acknowledge how we have strayed from who we want to be.

These things can be hard to do because we don't live in a society and culture that supports paying attention. In fact, everything around us tries to pull us away from paying attention to our true selves. But we have to be strong. We have to retrain ourselves and remain committed to the search.

What is the reward of being disciplined, learning more about ourselves, and remaining attentive to our thoughts, feelings, actions, and choices? Why do we really need self-awareness? We don't. Look around and you'll see that most people are unaware. Most people aren't paying attention. Most people are eternally distracted by the world around them.

We can survive without self-awareness. We can be successful. We can even be happy to a certain extent. But we can't be fully ourselves and fully alive. We can't experience the depths of joy, intimacy, authenticity, connection, peace, and fulfillment without constantly seeking self-awareness.

Once you practice self-questioning, you will no longer be satisfied with living on the surface of life or living a lie. As you gain more and more self-awareness, your experience of life will expand and improve exponentially. You will feel more centered, peaceful, and content.

I suggest you continue to ask yourself the questions in this book regularly, and notice your reactions to them and how your answers evolve over time. Continue writing your answers and the actions you take in a journal, and make notes about how your life has improved as a result of these questions. You might even keep an "action calendar" where you write down the specific actions you want to take each day in response to what you are learning about yourself.

If you find some of the questions raise painful, troubling, or confusing answers, consider working with a coach or counselor to navigate your feelings and to determine the best course of action.

Most importantly, remember to acknowledge the powerful inner work you are doing through self-questioning. By undertaking this process, you are claiming full responsibility for your life and happiness. That is something to be celebrated and to feel proud of. It is also incredibly empowering to realize that all of the answers you need reside inside of you and are accessible when you ask the right questions. You are the master of your destiny and the captain of your life.

Want to Learn More?

If you'd like to learn more about self-coaching, powerful questions, confidence, and other personal growth topics, please visit my blog **Live Bold and Bloom.com** for more articles, or check out my free video series on building your confidence at **SimpleSelfConfidence.com/free-videos.**

Did You Like
Self-Discovery Questions?

Thank you so much for purchasing *Self-Discovery Questions.* I'm honored by the trust you've placed in me and my work by choosing this book to improve your life. I truly hope you've enjoyed it and found it useful.

I'd like to ask you for a small favor. Would you please take just a minute to leave a review for this book on Amazon? This feedback will help me continue to write the kind of Kindle books that will best serve you. If you really loved the book, please let me know!

Other Books You Might Enjoy from Barrie Davenport

Confidence Building: Get Motivated, Overcome Social Fear, Be Assertive, and Empower Your Life for Success

Confidence Hacks: 99 Small Actions to Massively Boost Your Confidence

Sticky Habits: 6 Simple Steps to Create Good Habits that Stick

The 52-Week Life Passion Project

Peace of Mindfulness: Everyday Rituals to Conquer Anxiety and Claim Unlimited Inner Peace

48100741R10059

Made in the USA
Columbia, SC
06 January 2019